D1162875

THE OUTDOORS

FRESHWATER FISHING

by Tom Carpenter

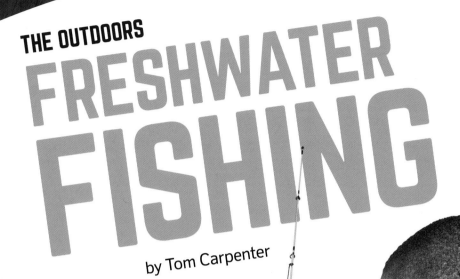

FOCUS
READERS

St. John the Baptist Parish Library
2920 Highway 51
LaPlace, LA 70068

WWW.FOCUSREADERS.COM

Copyright © 2018 by Focus Readers, Lake Elmo, MN 55042. All rights reserved. No part of this book may be reproduced or utilized in any form or by any means without written permission from the publisher.

Focus Readers is distributed by North Star Editions:
sales@northstareditions.com | 888-417-0195

Produced for Focus Readers by Red Line Editorial.

Photographs ©: IPGGutenbergUKLtd/iStockphoto, cover, 1; alexeys/iStockphoto, 4–5; Everett Collection/Shutterstock Images, 7; Dan Thornberg/Shutterstock Images, 8–9; wmaster890/iStockphoto, 10; bradwieland/iStockphoto, 13; princessdlaf/iStockphoto, 14 (top left); spxChrome/iStockphoto, 14 (top right); Denis Kot/iStockphoto, 14 (bottom left); Labrador Photo Video/Shutterstock Images, 14 (bottom right); Sergio Kumer/iStockphoto, 15 (top left); kyoshino/iStockphoto, 15 (top right); Pavel Lysenko/Shutterstock Images, 15 (bottom left); fotografermen/iStockphoto, 15 (bottom right); Kletr/Shutterstock Images, 16–17; Keith Szafranski/iStockphoto, 19; stammphoto/iStockphoto, 20; 18042011/Shutterstock Images, 22–23; Suzanne Tucker/Shutterstock Images, 25; waldru/iStockphoto, 26–27; CribbVisuals/iStockphoto, 28

ISBN
978-1-63517-230-0 (hardcover)
978-1-63517-295-9 (paperback)
978-1-63517-425-0 (ebook pdf)
978-1-63517-360-4 (hosted ebook)

Library of Congress Control Number: 2017935878

Printed in the United States of America
Mankato, MN
June, 2017

ABOUT THE AUTHOR

Tom Carpenter is a father, angler, and outdoor writer. He has fished the rivers, lakes, and creeks of the upper Midwest for more than 50 years. He has also guided many young anglers, including his three sons, to much fishing success. Tom grew up fishing in Wisconsin, but now his home base is near the shores of Bass Lake, Minnesota.

TABLE OF CONTENTS

CHAPTER 1

FRESHWATER ANGLING

The pond is glassy calm. You paddle your kayak toward a patch of lily pads near the shoreline. You pick up your rod and **cast** your **lure**. As you tug the line, the lure glides through the water. Suddenly, a largemouth bass bites it. There is a giant splash as you struggle to reel in the huge fish.

Ponds are good places to fish for largemouth bass and bluegills.

Today, **anglers** fish mostly for sport and adventure. But humans have fished for food for thousands of years. Some people used spears or wooden poles with sharpened points. They waded into shallow water, waited near holes in the ice, or rode in boats.

Some people used nets. They placed nets made from reeds across streams. Other people wove nets from plant fibers. People cast these nets into lakes. Still others used hooks and lines. They often carved hooks from bone. Lines were made from hair or plant fibers.

The first fishing rods and reels were invented in England in the 1600s. By

Fishing poles have changed a lot over the years.

the 1700s, fishing reels often included gears and handles. Rods were made from flexible bamboo instead of stiff wood. Silk fishing line replaced woven horsehair. European settlers brought these fishing tools to North America. Since then, fishing equipment has continued to improve.

CHAPTER 2

RODS, REELS, AND RIGS

People go freshwater fishing in streams, rivers, lakes, and ponds. Unlike the ocean, these bodies of water are not salty. That is why they are known as freshwater.

Many people fish from boats with motors. Others paddle kayaks or canoes. These smaller boats are better for fishing in small streams or ponds.

Anglers choose their bait and fishing method based on which fish they hope to catch.

Lures can be designed to look like minnows, tadpoles, or crayfish.

Anglers use a variety of equipment to catch fish. Fishing rods are long poles. Anglers use rods to cast their bait. A reel is attached to the rod. The reel holds the fishing line. At the end of the line is the bait or lure. Lures look like insects or animals that fish eat. Some lures flash or rattle to attract fish.

Many anglers use live bait. Minnows, worms, and leeches are popular choices. Anglers carry live bait in buckets or insulated boxes. When an angler fishes with live bait, he or she sets up a rig.

FISHING LURES

There are many types of artificial lures. Jigs are hooks with heavy, painted heads. They bring bait down into the water to where the fish are. Spinners and spinner baits have flashing blades that help attract fish. Some lures are designed to imitate a fish's **prey**. For example, lures known as spoons are painted, flashy pieces of metal. They move in the water like injured baitfish.

A rig is the combination of hook, sinker, and other equipment at the end of the line. A sinker pulls the line down into the water. A swivel prevents the line from twisting and snarling. Sometimes anglers use floats or bobbers, too. Floats and bobbers go underwater when a fish bites. Anglers often carry their hooks, sinkers, lures, and other equipment in a tackle box. They may use a net to **land** fish that they have reeled in.

Freshwater anglers use several methods. Casting is when an angler tosses out a lure and reels it back in. Still fishing is another method. The angler casts the bait but does not reel it back in.

Trolling anglers may cover a lot of water to find fish.

Instead, the angler lets the bait sit in one spot. When trolling, an angler lets out the bait or lure behind a boat. Then the angler pulls the bait along as the boat moves slowly.

FRESHWATER FISHING SUPPLIES

☐ 1. Bait container

☐ 2. Bobber

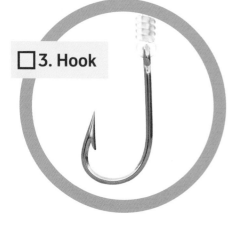

☐ 3. Hook

☐ 4. Landing net

☐ 5. Rod and reel

☐ 6. Sinker

☐ 7. Stringer

☐ 8. Tackle box

CHAPTER 3

FROM STRATEGY TO STRINGER

Freshwater anglers choose their fishing locations based on the kind of fish they hope to catch. For example, largemouth bass often live in weedy, shallow water. Smallmouth bass can typically be found near rocks in the water. Weeds, stumps, and rocks are also good places to find small fish called panfish.

Northern pike tend to swim near rocks and weeds.

Panfish species include sunfish, crappies, and perch. These fish spend most of their time hiding from bigger fish. Worms, grubs, and minnows make good bait for catching panfish.

Anglers also pursue large **predator** fish such as walleyes, catfish, and pike. A walleye's big eyes help it see and hunt in the dark. For this reason, many anglers fish for walleyes at night. Catfish hunt at night, too. They can be found in rivers and streams.

When a fish bites, the angler must set the hook before reeling in the line. Pulling the rod upward causes the hook to catch

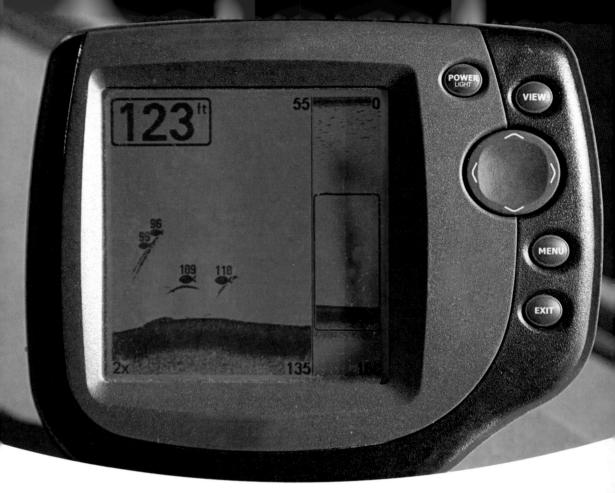

A fish finder uses sound waves to locate fish swimming near an angler's boat.

in the fish's mouth. Otherwise, the hook would slide out.

Once the hook is set, the fish often jumps or tugs on the line. The angler must pull against the fish to reel it in.

Bass can be found all across North America.

This is known as playing the fish. A skilled angler keeps the line tight while steadily reeling in the fish.

Some anglers keep and eat their catches. They put the fish on a stringer in the water or on ice in a cooler. This helps keep the fish fresh. Anglers clean the fish before bringing them home to cook.

Other anglers prefer catch-and-release fishing. After these anglers reel in a fish, they gently let it go back into the water.

CLEANING A FISH

Some anglers **fillet** a fish to clean it. Using a sharp and flexible knife, they slice the fish's meat away from its bones. Then they trim off the skin. Filleted fish is cooked in pieces without bones. Other anglers prefer to cook the fish whole. First, they scale the fish. Then they remove its **entrails**. The fish's bones are removed after cooking, when the fish is being eaten.

St. John the Baptist Parish Library
2920 Highway 51
LaPlace, LA 70068

CHAPTER 4

WATER SAFETY

Freshwater anglers spend a lot of time in and around the water. The water may have strong currents. The currents could cause wading anglers to fall and get hurt. Many anglers keep a first aid kit nearby. That way, they have bandages and medicine in case of cuts or other injuries.

Many harbors have first aid kits or life preservers in case of accidents.

Freshwater anglers should wear life jackets or other personal flotation devices. These can help prevent drowning if anglers fall into the water.

Sometimes the water is so cold that a person who falls in could pass out. Currents in deeper water could also prevent the person from swimming to shore. A life jacket helps the person stay afloat. It holds the person's head above the water so that he or she can breathe.

Wearing sunscreen is important, too. The sun reflects off the water, making it easy for anglers to get sunburned. Sunglasses protect an angler's eyes from the sun's glare. Some sunglasses have

It is important that children wear life jackets at all times when on a boat.

polarized lenses. These lenses cut the glare from the water's surface. This allows an angler to see down into the water. A wide-brimmed hat can keep the sun off an angler's face and neck as well.

CHAPTER 5

PROTECTING FISH HABITATS

Laws and limits protect fish and their **habitats**. Fishing seasons are specific dates when people are allowed to fish. A bag limit tells how many fish a person can keep each day. People must buy a fishing license for the state or province where they are fishing.

Money from fishing licenses is used to maintain the fish's habitats.

Anglers should not keep a fish out of water for very long.

Anglers can also protect fish by following four catch-and-release guidelines. First, anglers should play each fish quickly so it does not get too tired. Second, they should make sure their hands are wet whenever they pick up a fish. This keeps the fish's slime coating intact.

Third, anglers should remove hooks gently. If a hook is deep in a fish's mouth, they should not try to dig it out. Instead, they should cut the line near the hook. The fish's body fluids will later dissolve the hook. Fourth, anglers should hold the fish gently in the water before releasing it so the fish can rest before swimming off.

BARBLESS HOOKS

Most hooks have a sharp point called a barb. The barb helps the hook stick firmly in the fish's mouth. But it can hurt the fish. Barbless hooks do not have this sharp point. Anglers who use barbless hooks might lose more fish when reeling them in. But barbless hooks make releasing fish easier.

FOCUS ON
FRESHWATER FISHING

Write your answers on a separate piece of paper.

1. Write a sentence that explains the main idea of Chapter 3.

2. If you caught a fish, would you keep it or release it? Why?

3. What should an angler do if a hook is deep in a fish's mouth?

   A. use a pliers to dig out the hook
   B. cut the line near the hook
   C. tie a knot in the line before pulling out the hook

4. Why might anglers who use barbless hooks lose more fish while reeling them in?

   A. Without a barb, the hook can more easily slide out of the fish's mouth.
   B. Without a barb, the hook cannot hold any bait.
   C. Without a barb, the hook can more easily rip through the fish's skin.

Answer key on page 32.

GLOSSARY

anglers
People who fish with a rod, reel, and line.

cast
To use a fishing rod to throw a line with bait or a lure out over the water.

entrails
An animal's internal organs.

fillet
To cut meat into thin strips that have no bones.

habitats
The type of places where plants or animals normally grow or live.

land
To bring in a hooked fish from the water.

lure
An artificial bait used to attract and catch fish.

predator
An animal that hunts other animals for food.

prey
An animal that is hunted and killed by another animal for food.

TO LEARN MORE

BOOKS

Carpenter, Tom. *Freshwater Fishing: Bass, Trout, Walleye, Catfish, and More.* Minneapolis: Lerner, 2013.

Cermele, Joe. *The Total Fishing Manual: 317 Essential Fishing Skills.* San Francisco, CA: Weldon Owen, 2017.

Howard, Melanie A. *Freshwater Fishing for Kids.* North Mankato, MN: Capstone Press, 2013.

NOTE TO EDUCATORS

Visit **www.focusreaders.com** to find lesson plans, activities, links, and other resources related to this title.

INDEX

Answer Key: 1. Answers will vary; **2.** Answers will vary; **3.** B; **4.** A

THE NFL AT
A GLANCE

AWESOME NFL RECORDS
12 HARD-TO-REACH MARKS

by Matt Tustison

www.12StoryLibrary.com

Copyright © 2016 by Peterson Publishing Company, North Mankato, MN 56003. All rights reserved. No part of this book may be reproduced or utilized in any form or by any means without written permission from the publisher.

12-Story Library is an imprint of Peterson Publishing Company and Press Room Editions.

Produced for 12-Story Library by Red Line Editorial

Photographs ©: Morry Gash/AP Images, cover, 1, 22, 23; Pro Football Hall of Fame/AP Images, 4; Mark Humphrey/AP Images, 5; AP Images, 6, 12, 29; Harold P. Matosian/AP Images, 9; NFL Photos/AP Images, 10, 18; Lennox McLendon/AP Images, 14, 28; Andrew Innerarity/AP Images, 15; Kevin Higley/AP Images, 17; Tony Gutierrez/AP Images, 19; Lenny Ignelzi/AP Images, 21; Chris Carlson/AP Images, 24; Kevin Terrell/AP Images, 25; Jack Dempsey/AP Images, 26

ISBN
978-1-63235-156-2 (hardcover)
978-1-63235-196-8 (paperback)
978-1-62143-248-7 (hosted ebook)

Library of Congress Control Number: 2015934301

Printed in the United States of America
Mankato, MN
June, 2015

Go beyond the book. Get free, up-to-date content on this topic at 12StoryLibrary.com.

TABLE OF CONTENTS

1

GREEN BAY PACKERS CAPTURE MOST NFL TITLES

The Green Bay Packers are older than the National Football League (NFL). E. L. "Curly" Lambeau founded the team in 1919. That was one year before the NFL's first season. Green Bay joined the league in 1921. Lambeau was the Packers' first coach. He also played tailback for the team from 1921 to 1929.

In his last year as a player-coach, Lambeau led the Packers to their first championship. As a coach, he led them to titles in 1930, 1931, 1936, 1939, and 1944, as well.

The Packers struggled after Lambeau left in 1949. But a new dynasty began when Vince Lombardi took over as coach in 1959. The team featured hall of fame players such as quarterback Bart Starr. He guided them to NFL titles in 1961, 1962, and 1965. They also won the first two Super Bowls. The games were held after the 1966 and 1967 seasons. Green Bay became known as "Titletown, USA." After Lombardi's death in 1970, the NFL renamed the Super Bowl trophy the Vince Lombardi Trophy.

Curly Lambeau in 1919

Aaron Rodgers celebrates after leading the Packers to victory in Super Bowl XLV.

No team could match the Packers' success. A 1991 trade for quarterback Brett Favre began a new era of success. Favre helped Green Bay win the Super Bowl after the 1996 season. It was the Packers' first NFL title in 29 years. Then quarterback Aaron Rodgers led another title run in the 2010 season. Rodgers guided Green Bay past the Pittsburgh Steelers 31–25 in Super Bowl XLV. The win gave the Packers a record 13 championships. The Lombardi Trophy was back in Green Bay.

"That is where it belongs," Packers linebacker A. J. Hawk said.

THINK ABOUT IT

Nine of the Packers championships came in the era before the Super Bowl. Meanwhile, all six of the Pittsburgh Steelers' titles came in the Super Bowl era. Should the Packers still be considered the NFL's most successful team? Why or why not?

9

NFL championships won by the Chicago Bears, second only to the Green Bay Packers.

- All but one of the Bears' championships came before the Super Bowl era.
- The Pittsburgh Steelers lead all teams with six Super Bowl wins.

5

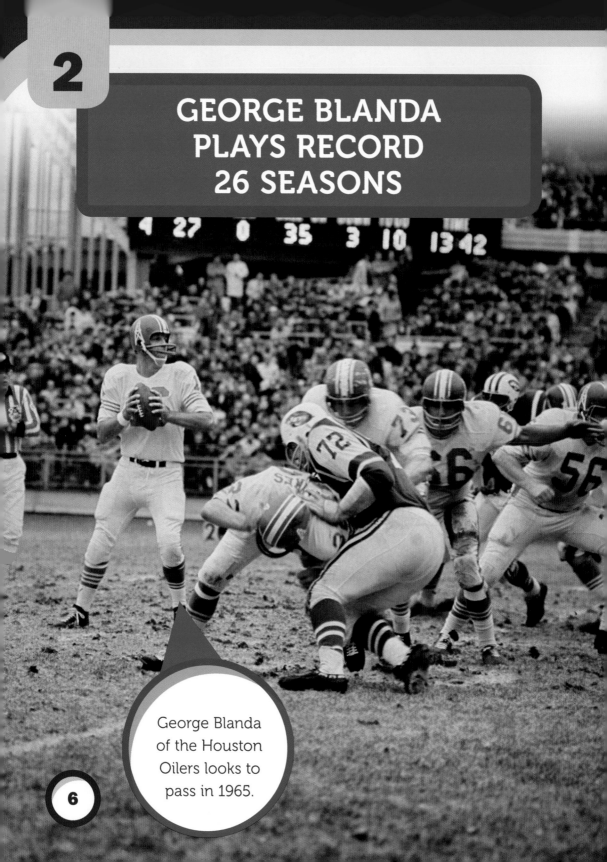

2

GEORGE BLANDA PLAYS RECORD 26 SEASONS

George Blanda
of the Houston
Oilers looks to
pass in 1965.

36

George Blanda's touchdown passes in 1961. This stood as a pro football record until 1984.

- The AFL and NFL merged in 1970.
- Blanda won the AFL Most Valuable Player (MVP) Award in 1961.

HOT STRETCH AT AGE 43

In 1970, the 43-year-old George Blanda had an amazing stretch. In a five-game stretch, he provided the Raiders with four wins and one tie. Each one came on a last-second touchdown pass or field goal.

The Chicago Bears signed 21-year-old George Blanda in 1949. No one could have predicted how long he'd play.

Blanda began as a quarterback and placekicker for the Bears. He became the team's top quarterback in 1953. But a shoulder injury the next year set him back. He would serve mainly as a kicker the next four seasons.

Blanda retired after the 1958 season. But he returned to pro football in 1960. Only he didn't come back to the NFL. Instead he signed with the Houston Oilers of the new American Football League (AFL). The AFL was a rival league to the NFL. Blanda became the Oilers' quarterback and placekicker. He

helped Houston win the AFL's first two titles in 1960 and 1961.

In March 1967, the Oilers released Blanda. But the AFL's Oakland Raiders signed him. He was a successful kicker and backup quarterback for another nine seasons.

Blanda finally retired before the 1976 season. He was nearly 49 years old. And he had played an amazing 26 seasons. No other player has matched that. Over those 26 seasons, Blanda threw 236 touchdown passes and scored 2,002 points. The points total was a record at the time. Blanda's points came from nine rushing touchdowns, 335 field goals, and 943 extra points.

3

"NIGHT TRAIN" LANE GRABS 14 INTERCEPTIONS IN 1952

Dick "Night Train" Lane was a rookie in 1952. Back then, the NFL's regular season was just 12 games instead of the 16 played today. Teams did not pass as often during Lane's playing days either. Yet he still managed to grab 14 interceptions that year. That still stands as the NFL single-season record.

Lane had served four years in the army. He wanted to be a wide receiver when he showed up to try out for the Los Angeles Rams in 1952. The defending NFL champions were impressed by Lane's skills. But they already had future hall-of-fame wide receivers in Tom Fears and Elroy "Crazy Legs" Hirsch. They put Lane at cornerback.

Fears helped Lane learn concepts such as pass patterns and defensive schemes. Fears played music during these tutoring sessions. One of his favorite songs was the hit record "Night Train." Ben Sheets, Fears's roommate, started calling Lane "Night Train." The nickname stuck.

"Night Train" was traded to the Chicago Cardinals in 1954. He spent six years in Chicago and six more seasons with the Detroit Lions. Lane retired after the 1965 season. He picked off 68 passes in his career. Only three players had more through 2014.

2

Seasons in which Dick "Night Train" Lane led the NFL in interceptions.

- Lane was named first team All-Pro three times.
- He was selected to seven Pro Bowls.

The Los Angeles Rams' Dick "Night Train" Lane intercepts a pass against the Green Bay Packers in 1952.

4

1972 DOLPHINS ACHIEVE A PERFECT SEASON

In 2007, the New England Patriots went 16–0 in the regular season. Then they won two playoff games. In the Super Bowl, however, they lost to the New York Giants. Members of the 1972 Miami Dolphins celebrated as they always do. The Patriots' loss meant the '72 Dolphins remained the NFL's only undefeated team in the Super Bowl era.

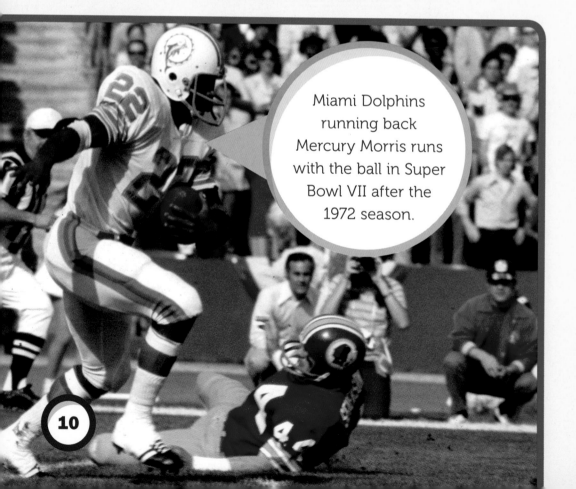

Miami Dolphins running back Mercury Morris runs with the ball in Super Bowl VII after the 1972 season.

DON SHULA: THE NFL'S LEADER IN COACHING WINS

In 1970, the Miami Dolphins hired Don Shula away from the Baltimore Colts. Shula had been a top coach with the Colts since 1963. With the Dolphins, he continued his success. Shula guided the team to five Super Bowls from 1970 to 1995. The Dolphins won twice. He finished his NFL coaching career with a 347–173–6 record, including playoff games. No coach has won more games.

The '72 Dolphins finished the regular season 14–0. A 14–7 win over the Washington Redskins in Super Bowl VII capped a 17–0 overall record. Teams such as the Patriots have come close to matching the Dolphins' perfect season. None have succeeded.

1

NFL ranking on offense and defense for the 1972 Dolphins.

- The Dolphins scored an average of 27.5 points per game.
- Opponents averaged just 12.2 points per game against Miami.

In 1972, Miami had future hall of famers such as quarterback Bob Griese and running back Larry Csonka. But other, lesser-known players often made the difference. The Dolphins featured a defense that lacked star power. It was known as the "No-Name Defense."

The offense received help from unsung heroes, too. Griese broke his leg in the fifth game. Earl Morrall, Miami's 38-year-old backup, came off the bench and kept the unbeaten streak alive. Griese returned in the American Football Conference title game. He led Miami past the Pittsburgh Steelers 21–17. Two weeks later, Griese and the Dolphins were Super Bowl champions.

11

5

ERIC DICKERSON RUSHES FOR 2,105 YARDS IN 1984

The Los Angeles Rams chose running back Eric Dickerson second overall in the 1983 NFL Draft.

He set NFL rookie records for most rushing yards (1,808) and touchdowns (18). And he was just

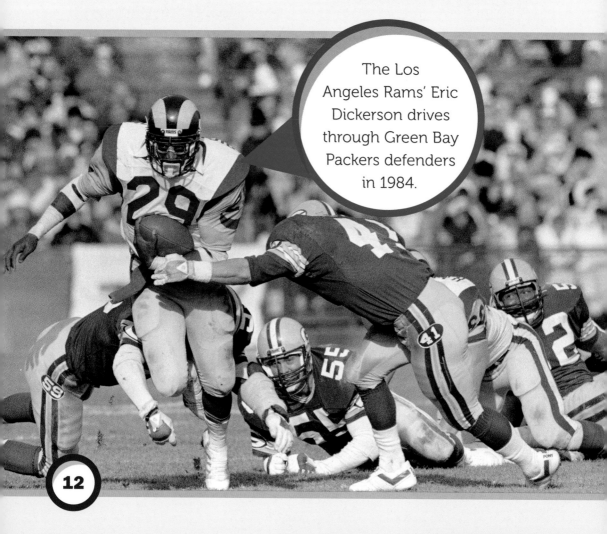

The Los Angeles Rams' Eric Dickerson drives through Green Bay Packers defenders in 1984.

12

Games with more than 100 rushing yards for Eric Dickerson in 1984. This was an NFL single-season record at the time.

- The Minnesota Vikings' Adrian Peterson nearly broke Dickerson's record in 2012.
- Peterson ran for 2,097 yards. He was less than a first down from the record.

THINK ABOUT IT

Today's NFL season is 16 games. It wasn't always that long, however. Until 1978, teams only played 14 games. Some seasons were even shorter in the NFL's early days. How should fans view records set in a 16-game season as compared to those set in shorter seasons? Are they all equal?

getting started. The next season, Dickerson ran for 2,105 yards. That broke the mark of 2,003 set by O. J. Simpson in 1973. However, Simpson's achievement came in a 14-game season. In Dickerson's era, the season was 16 games long.

Five other NFL running backs have reached 2,000 yards rushing since 1984. But none has equaled Dickerson's total.

Dickerson was one of the best pure runners the NFL has ever seen. He was known for his upright running style. Dickerson was also remembered for wearing his prescription goggles on the field. He needed them to correct his poor vision.

In 1986, Dickerson earned a third rushing title. The Rams traded Dickerson to the Indianapolis Colts in 1987. The next year, he won his fourth rushing crown. During his 11-year career, Dickerson ran for 13,259 yards. This was the second most ever at the time of his retirement.

6

JERRY RICE SETS WIDE RECEIVER STANDARDS

Jerry Rice's name dominates the NFL's receiving records. His career marks include most receptions (1,549), receiving yards (22,895), touchdown catches (197), and total touchdowns (208).

The San Francisco 49ers selected Rice in the first round of the 1985 NFL Draft. Rice was already a star by his second season. He had 86 catches in 1986. His 1,570 receiving yards and 15 touchdowns were NFL highs. That season also began a streak of 11 straight in which Rice had at least 1,000 receiving yards. In 1987, Rice had 22 touchdown catches. That was the NFL record at the time. And he did so while playing just 12 games.

Rice was a star in Super Bowls for the 49ers. He helped San Francisco win NFL titles after the 1988, 1989, and 1994 seasons. In those Super

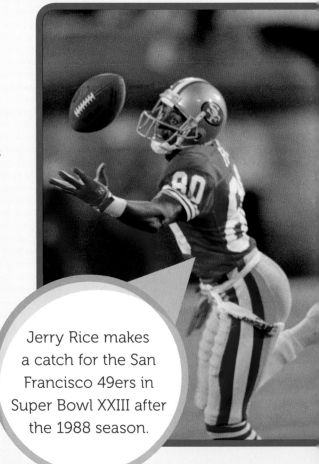

Jerry Rice makes a catch for the San Francisco 49ers in Super Bowl XXIII after the 1988 season.

Jerry Rice races for a touchdown in Super Bowl XXIX after the 1994 season.

14

Seasons in which Jerry Rice reached 1,000 receiving yards. This is an NFL record.

- Rice spent 16 of his 20 NFL seasons with the 49ers.
- In San Francisco, Rice caught passes from hall-of-fame quarterbacks Joe Montana and Steve Young.
- Rice ended his career with the Oakland Raiders and Seattle Seahawks.

Bowl victories, Rice had a combined 28 catches for 512 yards and seven touchdowns. Rice was named MVP in the first of those games, Super Bowl XXIII. San Francisco beat the Cincinnati Bengals 20–16 in that game.

THE BEST EVER?

In 2010, the NFL Network televised a series called "The Top 100: NFL's Greatest Players." A panel of experts chose Jerry Rice as the best player of all time.

7

BRUCE SMITH RECORDS 200 SACKS IN CAREER

Defensive players have been sacking quarterbacks as long as the NFL has been around. But the NFL has only been recording sacks since 1982. Since then, no player has as many quarterback sacks as defensive end Bruce Smith.

The Buffalo Bills picked Smith first overall in the 1985 draft. Smith was lightning fast and extremely strong. "He is so strong," said hall-of-fame quarterback Warren Moon, "that he can bulldoze over you."

In 1990, Smith recorded a career-high 19 sacks. He then helped lead Buffalo to its first of four straight Super Bowl appearances.

Smith was best known for his time with the Bills. But he was playing for the Washington Redskins on December 7, 2003. Washington was playing the New York Giants that day. Smith charged toward quarterback Jesse Palmer and brought him down for a 7-yard loss. It was his 199th sack. That broke Reggie White's career record of 198. Two weeks later, Smith recorded sack number 200. It was his final sack in his final season. He dropped Chicago Bears quarterback Rex Grossman for a 5-yard loss.

14.5

Bruce Smith's total sacks in the playoffs. That was an NFL record when he retired.

- Smith was named NFL Defensive Player of the Year in 1990 and 1996.
- Smith helped the Bills reach a record four Super Bowls in a row.

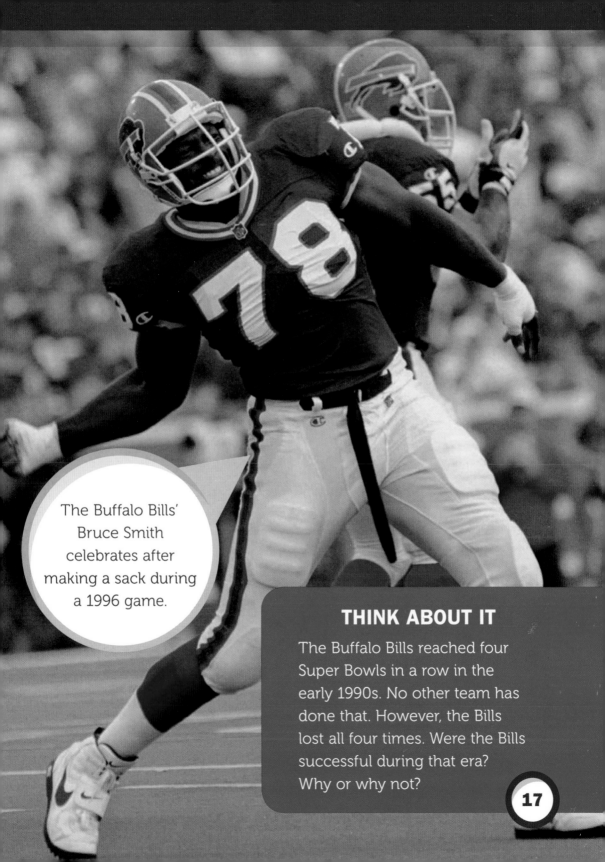

The Buffalo Bills' Bruce Smith celebrates after making a sack during a 1996 game.

THINK ABOUT IT

The Buffalo Bills reached four Super Bowls in a row in the early 1990s. No other team has done that. However, the Bills lost all four times. Were the Bills successful during that era? Why or why not?

8

EMMITT SMITH BREAKS THE CAREER RUSHING MARK

Emmitt Smith was tough. He was also consistent. It's no surprise that he is the league's career rushing champion.

Smith just missed the 1,000-yard rushing mark as a rookie for the Dallas Cowboys in 1990. He then went on a record run of 11 straight seasons with 1,000 yards on the ground. During this time, Smith helped the Cowboys become the NFL's most dominant team. Dallas won Super Bowls after the 1992, 1993, and 1995 seasons.

The Dallas Cowboys' Emmitt Smith runs against the Los Angeles Raiders in 1992.

In 2002, Smith rushed for 975 yards. But he made history on October 27 of that season. Smith entered that game against the Seattle Seahawks with 16,634 career rushing yards. He trailed former Chicago Bears star Walter Payton by 93 yards for the all-time record. Smith finished the game with 109 yards. This gave him 16,743 for his career. Payton's record of 16,726 had stood since the 1987 season.

Smith retired after the 2004 season. He finished his career with 18,355 rushing yards and an NFL-record 164 rushing touchdowns. Both marks still stand.

Emmitt Smith celebrates with a silver football trophy after setting the NFL career rushing record in 2002.

25
Rushing touchdowns for Emmitt Smith in 1995. It was an NFL record at the time.

- Smith led the NFL in rushing yards four times.
- He was the NFL MVP in 1993.
- He earned All-Pro honors four times.

ONE OF THE GREATEST COWBOYS

In 2012, ESPNDallas.com ranked the 50 greatest Cowboys players of all time. Emmitt Smith came in second, only behind quarterback Roger Staubach. Staubach was a star in the 1970s.

9

LADAINIAN TOMLINSON SCORES 31 TOUCHDOWNS

LaDainian Tomlinson was a touchdown-scoring machine in 2006 for the San Diego Chargers. Game after game, he bulldozed his way into the end zone. By his 13th game, the single-season record was in reach. The Seattle Seahawks' Shaun Alexander had set it just one year earlier with 28 touchdowns.

The Chargers hosted the Denver Broncos in that 13th game on December 10, 2006. "L. T." needed two touchdowns to tie Alexander. Instead he got three. Tomlinson scored on a 1-yard run early in the second quarter. Tomlinson later scored on a 6-yard run with 3:57 left. Then the Broncos quickly lost a fumble. Only 47 seconds after his 28th touchdown, Tomlinson scored his 29th touchdown on a 7-yard run.

Tomlinson's teammates carried him to the sideline. He had set the record. The Chargers' win clinched the division title. Tomlinson hoisted the ball in the air in one hand. With the other hand, he held up his index finger, signaling that he was No. 1.

But he was not yet finished. One week later, Tomlinson scored two more rushing touchdowns. His first score gave him 180 points for the season. That broke the mark of

3

Seasons (2004, 2006, 2007) in which LaDainian Tomlinson led the NFL in rushing touchdowns.

- Tomlinson rushed for an NFL-high 1,815 yards in that 2006 season.
- He was named the NFL MVP that season.

176. Green Bay Packers running back/kicker Paul Hornung had set it in 1960. Tomlinson's second touchdown was his 28th on the ground. That was also a record.

Tomlinson didn't score in either of the Chargers' last two games. But he finished the year with three single-season records while helping the Chargers go 14–2.

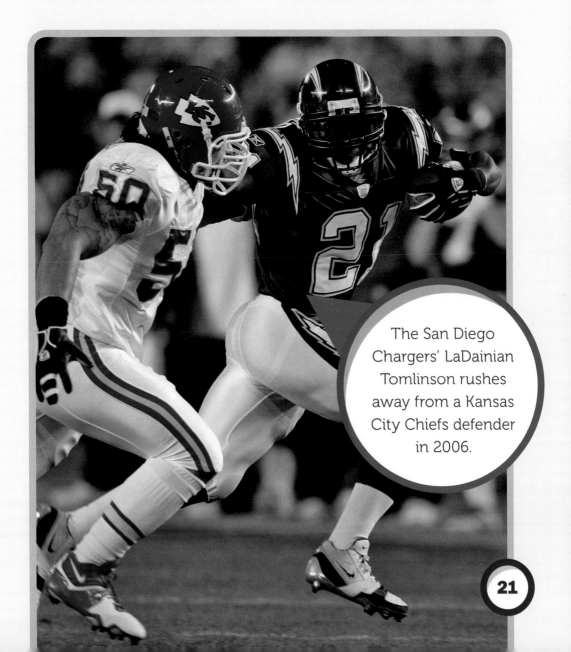

The San Diego Chargers' LaDainian Tomlinson rushes away from a Kansas City Chiefs defender in 2006.

10

BRETT FAVRE BECOMES THE NFL'S IRON MAN

The decision was announced Monday, December 13, 2010, on Twitter. "Vikings inactives—12, 19, 25, 31, 76, 90, 91 . . . and 4. The streak ends . . . "

Quarterback Brett Favre was No. 4. After a remarkable 297 consecutive starts over 19 seasons, he was sidelined. Favre had a shoulder injury too serious to overcome. He would miss Minnesota's 21–3 loss to the New York Giants.

Favre cherished that "Iron Man" record. It was set over 19 seasons, 16 of them with the Green Bay Packers. He had to play through various injuries. In December 2003, he played in a game the day after his father's sudden death. But he always played—and he almost always played well.

Green Bay Packers quarterback Brett Favre looks to pass in a 2006 game.

Favre launches a pass for the Packers in a 2006 game.

In that memorable 2003 game, Favre passed for 399 yards and four touchdowns. His inspired performance led Green Bay past the Oakland Raiders 41–7 on *Monday Night Football*.

Asked how to define toughness, Favre answered, "To play every week and to be someone that your teammates can rely on to be there for them."

3

Consecutive NFL MVP Awards Brett Favre won between 1995 and 1997. This is a record.

- Former Vikings defensive end Jim Marshall previously held the "Iron Man" record.
- Marshall had started 270 straight games from 1961 to 1979.

THE BEGINNING OF THE STREAK

On September 20, 1992, Packers quarterback Don Majkowski was injured. Favre came off the bench and threw a game-winning touchdown pass against the Cincinnati Bengals. He made his first start the next week. That began the consecutive starts streak.

11

DEVIN HESTER PUTS THE "SPECIAL" IN SPECIAL TEAMS

Devin Hester burst onto the scene as a rookie with the Chicago Bears in 2006. He returned three punts and two kickoffs for touchdowns. His play helped the Bears reach the Super Bowl. He then opened the game with a 92-yard kickoff return for a score. However, Chicago lost 29–17 to the Indianapolis Colts.

The next season, Hester returned four punts for touchdowns. That tied the NFL single-season record. He added two kickoff returns for scores. "When Devin gets the ball in his hands, he's magic," Bears linebacker Lance Briggs said of Hester in 2007.

He didn't slow down for many seasons. He played for the Bears

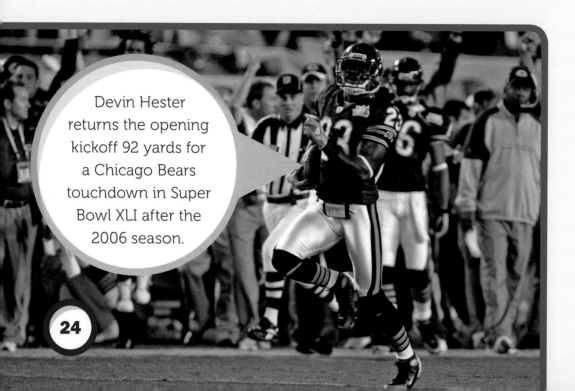

Devin Hester returns the opening kickoff 92 yards for a Chicago Bears touchdown in Super Bowl XLI after the 2006 season.

through the 2013 season. During that time, he returned 13 punts, five kickoffs, and one missed field goal for touchdowns. His 19 return touchdowns matched the record set by his idol, Deion Sanders.

In 2014, Hester joined Sanders's former team, the Atlanta Falcons. Sanders was at the Georgia Dome on September 18. The Falcons were playing the Tampa Bay Buccaneers. In that game, Hester returned a punt 62 yards for a touchdown. Sanders saluted Hester from the video board. The torch had been passed. Hester had proven to be the game's new master of returns.

The Atlanta Falcons' Devin Hester high-steps into the end zone for his 20th career touchdown return in a 2014 game.

17

Career touchdowns Devin Hester scored through 2014 on plays other than special teams returns. He had 16 touchdown catches and one touchdown run.

- Hester won the NFL Alumni Special Teams Player of the Year Award three times through 2014.
- He was named first-team All-Pro three times for his special-teams play.

12

PEYTON MANNING SETS A NEW PASSING MILESTONE

When a quarterback is as good as Brett Favre was and plays as long as Favre did, career passing records are sure to fall. And indeed, Favre threw for a record 508 career touchdowns in his 302 games. Then along came Peyton Manning.

Broncos quarterback Peyton Manning throws his 509th career touchdown pass in a 2014 game.

342

Passing yards per game for Peyton Manning in 2013, another NFL record.

- Before his neck injury, Manning played in all 256 games over 13 seasons for the Colts.
- He won five NFL MVP Awards through 2014 and was All-Pro seven times.

A RECORD-SETTING SEASON

Peyton Manning had a remarkable 2013 season for the Denver Broncos. He set single-season records for touchdown passes (55) and passing yards (5,477).

On October 19, 2014, the Denver Broncos' quarterback threw an eight-yard touchdown pass to Demaryius Thomas. It was Manning's 509th career touchdown pass. And he achieved it in only his 246th career game.

Setting the record in 2014 was especially sweet for Manning. Like Favre, he was known for never missing a game. He started every game from 1998 through 2010 for the Indianapolis Colts. Then he missed the entire 2011 season because of neck problems. At one point, he didn't know that he would be able to throw a football again. Some people thought his NFL career was over. But the Broncos gave Manning another chance. They signed him to be their starter for the 2012 season.

It paid off. Manning played some of the best football of his career in Denver. In 2013, he broke many single-season passing records and led the Broncos to the Super Bowl. One year later, at age 38, he set the career touchdown record.

"I'm very humbled. I'm very honored," said Manning, who had 530 touchdown passes through 2014. "I certainly think about how grateful I am for all the teammates and coaches that I've played with and played for throughout my career."

FUN FACTS AND STORIES

- In 1958, the Detroit Lions traded quarterback Bobby Layne to the Pittsburgh Steelers. Layne was not happy. The Lions had been a good team. They had won four championships, including ones in 1952, 1953, and 1957. No more, according to Layne. He said the Lions wouldn't win another championship for 50 years. Indeed they didn't. The 50-year stretch finally ended in 2008. But Layne's curse saved the worst for last. The Lions became the first NFL team to finish 0–16 that year.

- The Lions are the only team to go 0–16. But the Tampa Bay Buccaneers had an even worse run. They began play in 1976. After going 0–14, they lost their first 12 games in 1977. That 26-game losing streak is a record.

- Jim Marshall was one of the NFL's best defensive ends in the 1960s and 1970s. He recovered an NFL-record 29 fumbles. Yet he is most remembered for one gone wrong on October 25, 1964. The Minnesota Vikings' star picked up a fumble and began running. He kept running for 60 yards. Finally, he reached the end zone. Only he was in the wrong end zone. Marshall's play became known as the "wrong way run."

- The Chicago Bears and Washington Redskins played on November 17, 1940. Washington won 7–3. A few weeks later, the two teams met again. This time the NFL championship was on the line. And this time the Bears walloped the Redskins 73–0. It is the biggest margin of defeat in NFL history.

- The 2000 Baltimore Ravens' defense was simply dominant. They allowed only 165 points and 970 rushing yards. Those were records for a 16-game season. Yet the Ravens got even better in the playoffs. The defense allowed just one touchdown in four playoff games. It's no wonder they won the Super Bowl.

GLOSSARY

draft
An event held each year in which NFL teams select players who are new to the league.

dynasty
A team that wins several championships over a short period of time.

inactives
Players on a football team who do not dress to compete in a given game.

playoffs
Games at the end of the season that decide a champion. When a team loses in the playoffs, its season is over.

Pro Bowl
The NFL all-star game.

retire
To end one's football career, usually because of age.

rookie
A first-year player.

sack
A play in which a defensive player tackles the quarterback for a loss of yards.

schemes
Systems or plans for how to run an offense or defense.

special teams
The groups of players on a football team who take part in kickoffs, punts, and field goals.

tutoring
Private lessons.

FOR MORE INFORMATION

Books

Editors at the NFL. *NFL Record & Fact Book 2014 (Official National Football League Record and Fact Book)*. New York: NFL, 2014.

Editors of Sports Illustrated. *Sports Illustrated Football's Greatest*. New York: Sports Illustrated, 2012.

Editors of Sports Illustrated Kids. *Sports Illustrated Kids 1st and 10: Top 10 Lists of Everything in Football*. New York: Sports Illustrated Kids, 2012.

Garner, Joe, and Bob Costas. *100 Yards of Glory: The Greatest Moments in NFL History*. Boston: Houghton Mifflin Harcourt, 2011.

Websites

NFL Rush
www.nflrush.com

Pro Football Hall of Fame
www.profootballhof.com

Pro Football Reference
www.pro-football-reference.com

Sports Illustrated Kids
www.sikids.com

INDEX

About the Author

Matt Tustison is a sports copyeditor at the *Washington Post*. He has also worked as a sports copyeditor at other newspapers, including the *St. Paul Pioneer Press* and as an editor and writer of children's sports books at Red Line Editorial in Burnsville, Minnesota.

READ MORE FROM 12-STORY LIBRARY

Every 12-Story Library book is available in many formats, including Amazon Kindle and Apple iBooks. For more information, visit your device's store or 12StoryLibrary.com.